UITGAVEN VAN HET
NEDERLANDS HISTORISCH-ARCHAEOLOGISCH INSTITUUT TE İSTANBUL

Publications de l'institut historique et archéologique néerlandais de Stamboul

sous la direction de
A.A. KAMPMAN et Machteld J. MELLINK

NOTES ON THE KITĀB NAḌRAT AL-IGHRĪḌ OF AL-MUẒAFFAR AL-ḤUSAYNĪ

(MS Damat Ibrahim 963, Süleymaniye Kütüphanesi, Istanbul)

NOTES ON THE *KITĀB NAḌRAT AL-IGHRĪḌ* OF AL-MUẒAFFAR AL-ḤUSAYNĪ

(MS Damat Ibrahim 963, Süleymaniye Kütüphanesi, Istanbul)

by

S.A. BONEBAKKER

İSTANBUL
NEDERLANDS HISTORISCH-ARCHAEOLOGISCH INSTITUUT
IN HET NABIJE OOSTEN
1968

Printed in Belgium

TABLE OF CONTENTS

INTRODUCTION

The collection of notes brought together in this article is part of a series of similar collections all dealing with texts on Arabic literary theory. The first article appeared in Oriens, Vol. XIII-XIV (1961). It was followed by a summary of the contents of Ṣafadī's *Faḍḍ al-Khitām 'an at-Tawriya wa-'l-Istikhdām*. This summary, together with notes on chapters on the *tawriya* and related figures of speech from other texts appeared in 1966 in the form of a small monograph [1]. I should like to express my gratitude to the "Nederlandse Organisatie voor Zuiver Wetenschappelijk Onderzoek" (Z.W.O.), The Hague, for enabling me to visit Turkey and study the manuscripts discussed in these earlier publications and in the present article, and the National Foundation on the Arts and the Humanities, Washington D.C., for supporting me financially during my sabbatical leave in 1967-68. I also wish to thank the Turkish Ministry of Education, the Österreichische Nationalbibliothek, Mr. A. Regragui, Director of the Bibliothèque Générale in Rabat, and Mr. 'Ābid al-Fāsī, Director of the Library of the Qarawiyyīn Mosque in Fez for supplying me with microfilms quoted in this article. I feel greatly indebted to the "Nederlands Instituut voor het Nabije Oosten" for undertaking the publication of this study.

My chief reason for publishing a summary of the *Faḍḍ al-Khitām* rather than an edition of the text itself was that this text, taken as a whole, hardly justifies the effort and expense which such an undertaking would involve on the part of a Western editor and that it would be reasonable to expect that the text would be published some day by an Eastern scholar. The same applies to Ḥusaynī's *Naḍrat al-Ighrīḍ*. When I began collecting notes on this text, I believed that it would be worth while to publish several long excerpts. Later, when I was able to examine the manuscripts of Ḥātimī's *Ḥilyat al-Muḥāḍara* in Fez, I found that, as I had long suspected, those passages which had a bearing on the early history of rhetorical terminology and constituted the chief interest of the *Naḍra* had, with two exceptions, all been borrowed from Ḥātimī and should therefore be published rather as part of a discussion of this important text. Moreover I decided that the numerous anecdotes in the *Naḍra*, on the analysis of which I had spent a considerable amount of time, did not really belong in an article which was meant to assess the importance of a particular text on rhetoric compared

---

1 S. A. Bonebakker, *Some Early Definitions of the Tawriya and Ṣafadī's Faḍḍ al-Xitām 'an at-Tawriya wa-'l-Istixdām* (Publications in Near and Middle East Studies, Columbia University, Series A, VIII).

with other similar works [2]. The notes here published therefore offer mainly a description of what appears to be the most important manuscript of the *Naḍra*, an attempt to trace the origin of its chapters on rhetoric, and an analysis of some problems of textual criticism. They will show that the *Naḍra*, by virtue of the numerous quotations it contains, can in some cases be used to reconstruct earlier and more important texts.

---

[2] For the same reason I will not publish the references I collected for the verse examples in the passages quoted in this article. Most of these verse examples are well known and can easily be identified in various dīwāns and anthologies. The passages quoted from the *Ḥilyat al-Muḥāḍara* of Ḥātimī, and in particular the early traditions on rhetorical terminology in this text, will be dealt with somewhat more fully in a forthcoming article, which will also contain those references that are important for the history of these traditions.

I. THE MS DAMAT IBRAHIM 963

The reason for limiting myself to the Damat Ibrahim manuscript as the only authority for the text of Ḥusaynī's *Naḍrat al-Ighrīd fī Nuṣrat al-Qarīḍ*, leaving aside the numerous other manuscripts mentioned by Brockelmann (*GAL*, G I, 282; S I, 496) is that it is the oldest manuscript available, and was written during the author's lifetime and studied under him. A second early manuscript in the Österreichische Nationalbibliothek (of which I examined a microfilm) appears to be several centuries younger. All other manuscripts mentioned by Brockelmann carry later dates, or have to be considered late manuscripts on the basis of the descriptions in various catalogues, with the exception of a manuscript in Mosul of which no detailed description exists. The following is a list of these manuscripts, the titles of the catalogues or periodicals where they have been described, and the dates or the approximate period in which they were written:

Aşır Ef. 937 : *MFO*, V (1911), 514. The MS may date from the 11th century.

Berlin 7174 : W. Ahlwardt, *Verzeichniss*, VI (1894), 358. Around 1100.

British Museum 1055 : *Catalogus codd. mss. or.*, Pars II, Vol. 3 (London, 1871), 477. MS dated 1140.

Cairo 1865 : *Fihrist Dār al-Kutub al-Miṣriyya*, III (Cairo, 1345/1927), 413. MS in *ta'līq* script, no date.

Hamidiye 1209 : *ZA*, XXVII (1912), 158. MS dated 1123.

Mawṣil 23 (not 22 as in *GAL*) : Dāwūd al-Čelebī al-Mawṣilī, *Makhṭūṭāt al-Mawṣil* (Baghdad, 1346), p. 42. No date.

Paris 1303 : De Slane, *Catalogue* (Paris, 1883-1895), p. 248. MS dated 1039-1040.

Paris 4236[3] : ibid., p. 681. MS dated 1039.

Paris 4420[1] : ibid., p. 703. MS dated 1100.

Rabat D1003[2] : *Hespéris*, XII (1931), 119; I.S. Allouche and A. Regragui, *Catalogue des manuscrits arabes de Rabat*, II (1958), 55. MS dated 1313.

Vienna 224 : G. Flügel, *Die Ar., Pers. und Türk. Handschriften*, I, (Vienna, 1865), 203. No date.

The main characteristics of the Damat Ibrahim manuscript are the following : Red leather binding; 242 written folios of 24 by 16.5 cms[1]; old, calligraphic,

[1] These measurements were supplied by the photographer. I forgot to make a note of the colour of the paper and the ink, which, as far as I can remember, are the yellowish white and dark brown often found in manuscripts of this period.

almost completely pointed and vocalized *naskhī*, 11 lines to the page (except 161a which has 16 lines and 161b which has 14 lines). Few marginal and interlinear notes, some of which are clearly in a handwriting different from that of the scribe and in some cases certainly of a much later date than the manuscript itself [2].

Fol. 1a (title page). Title :

كتاب / نضرة الاغريض فى نصرة القريض / تاليف العبد المشفق من ذنبه الراجى رحمة / ربه ابى على المظفر بن السعيد [3] ابى القاسم / الفضل بن ابى جعفر يحيى بن ابى على عبد الله / بن ابى عبد الله جعفر العلوى الحسينى / عفا الله عنه /

The title page contains several verse quotations, notes, and ex-libris. The ex-libris are almost illegible in the microfilm and I have made no attempt to identify them.

Fol. 1b (first page of the text). Incipit :

بسم الله الرحمان الرحيم وبه توفيقى / قال العبد المشفق من ذنبه الراجى رحمة / ربه ابو على المظفر بن السعيد ابى القسم / الفضل بن ابى جعفر يحيى بن ابى على / عبد الله بن ابى عبد الله جعفر / العلوى الحسينى / الحمد لله الباهرة آياته القاهرة سطواته القديم احسانه / العظيم سلطانه ....

Fol. 241a (last page of the text). Explicit :

... / وحيث انتهى بنا الكلام الى هذه الغاية واتينا فيها اشترطناه / بالكفاية والزيادة على الكفاية فقد وجب ان نختم الكتاب / ونقصر الاسهاب والله الموفق للصواب / ان شاء الله تعالى /

2 Those notes which are in the handwriting of the scribe appear to be mostly additions, some of which may have been made at the time the manuscript was studied under its author. There are also some notes marked خ which, since all or most of them appear in the verse examples, may be variant readings found in the various dīwāns and anthologies from which the author drew his material.

3 Brockelmann erroneously gives the term *as-sa'īd* (probably a synonym of *al-marḥūm*) as a proper name.

The rest of the page is taken up by the following interesting note :

تصفح هذا الجوهر المصون والدرّ المكنون الملتجئ الى حرم / الله تعالى الحسن

بن محمد بن الحسن الصغانى سمع الله دعاءه اذا / دعاه واعاده الى جناب حرمه وذراه من

مفتتحه الى مختتمه تصفح / منقّب وحصل منه على كل لؤلؤ منظّم ودرّ مثقّب والحمد

لله وحده وكفى / والصلوة على سيدنا محمد المصطفى وعلى اله والسلام /

which indicates that the manuscript was perused by the famous philologist Ṣaghānī, author of *the ʿUbāb az-Zākhir wa-'l-Lubāb al-Fākhir* [4]. The colophon continues on fol. 241b. Though undoubtedly by the same hand, this second part of the colophon shows a *dīwānī* type of calligraphy different from the rest of the text :

نجز الكتاب والحمد لله رب العلمين وصلواته / على سيدنا محمد نبيه واله الطاهرين /

على يد العبد الفقير الى رحمة الله وغفرانه / محمد بن حبش بن عبد السلم المراغى

الكاتب / عفا الله عنه بمدينة السلم حرسها الله / فى العشر الاوسط من شهر

شعبان سنة / اربعين (؟) [و]ستمأة /

It is not certain how we have to read the year in this colophon. The letters, *bā'*, *ʿayn*, *yā'*, and *nūn* are clear, but they are preceded by what looks like an *alif* and two *rā'*s, and a symbol which is no longer legible [5]. I have not been able to

---

4 Brockelmann, *GAL*, G I, 360; S I, 613. An interesting manuscript of the *ʿUbāb* not mentioned by Brockelmann is nº 2835 of the library of H. M. the King of Morocco, which the librarian, Mr. Muḥammad al-Mannūnī, kindly brought to my attention. It consists of Vol. XIII (roots يعط — غبض), Vol. XIV (زغف — قفزع), Vol. XV (خوق — زقف), and an unnumbered volume (فردس — بلع). Though I did not find time to examine the manuscript in detail, I established that the larger part of these four volumes is in the handwriting of Ṣaghānī, the rest having been substituted by a later hand. Vols. XIII, XIV, and XV have colophons in Ṣaghānī's handwriting : Vol. XIV carries the date Saturday, 13 Dhu 'l-Qaʿda, 649; Vol. XV the date Saturday, 24 Muḥarram, 650; and in Vol. XIII the date is no longer legible. The unnumbered volume has no colophon.

5 If we follow the MS Aşir Ef. 937 of the *Naḍra* (I briefly examined this manuscript in 1957) we should read 640. A note in the colophon of this manuscript states that it was copied from an original which had been studied under the author (نسخة مقروءة على مصنفها), which could very well mean that it was copied from the Damat Ibrahim manuscript. It also states that this original was written in 640.

identify the scribe in any of the collections of biographies at my disposal. The rest of the page is taken up by a reader's note which contains the name of one ʿAlī b. al-Makhlad, whom, as in the case of the scribe, I have not been able to identify.

Fol. 242a, which is the last written page of the manuscript, contains a *samāʿ* note [6]. This note is almost illegible on the microfilm. The following is an attempt to transcribe it with the help of the notes I made more than ten years ago :

قرات هذا الكتاب من مفتتحه (؟) الى مختتمه على مؤلفه المولى السيد الصدر
الكبير / شمس الدين ابى على المظفر بن الفضل ادام الله علوه وسمع بقرأتى
كملا / الامير ناصر الدين نصر بن على بن نصر الحارثى والولد النجب فلك الدين
حبش (؟) بن الامير / وسمع جماعة لم يكمل لهم السماع منهم فخر الدين على بن
الحسين / بن خشرم وشمس الدين على بن يحيى بن على الزرباطى (؟) ورشيد الدين /
يحيى بن محمد بن زيد المشهدى والسيد ابو عبد الله بن على المعروف بابن حمدان /
/ واجاز لهم ما فاتهم (in the margin :) / وذلك فى مجالس اخرها يوم الاربعاء رابع
عشرى شعبان سنة اثنين واربعين / وستمائة (؟) والحمد .... (rest illegible) /
وكتب الفقير الى رحمة الله وغفرانه / محمد بن حبش (؟) الكاتب عفا الله عنه /
بالتاريخ /

I have not succeeded in identifying any of the names in this *samāʿ* note, even with the help of the photographs of Ṣafadī's *Wāfī bi-'l-Wafayāt* in the Fondazione Caetani in Rome. If my reading of the last name is correct, the author of the note and the scribe who copied the manuscript would be the same person. The high quality of the manuscript shows that this scribe was a person of considerable scholarly ability, and it is therefore reasonable to assume that he was admitted to Ḥusaynī's circle.

A manuscript not mentioned by Brockelmann is no. 4464 of the Aḥmadiyya

Ḥājjī Khalīfa, however, gives 642 as the date of the composition of the *Naḍra* (*Kashf aẓ-Ẓunūn*, ed. Flügel, VI, 354).

6 On fol. 142a there is a *balāgh* note which may refer to this *samāʿ*. It contains no date and I have not discovered any similar notes in the manuscript.

Library in the Zaytūna in Tunis. The most important characteristics of this manuscript are the following : Modern cardboard binding; black ink on white paper; modern, not particularly beautiful, but readable, pointed and partially vocalized, Eastern *naskhī*, 21-23 lines to the page. The binding is somewhat loose, but otherwise the manuscript is in a good state of preservation. The pages are unnumbered : I counted 116. Beginning and end as in the Damat Ibrahim manuscript. The colophon carries the date 5 (يوم الخميس [sic]) Muḥarram 1104 and the note كتب من نسخة قرئت على المصنف رحمه الله which could mean that this manuscript was, like the MS Aşir Ef. 937 [7], copied from the Damat Ibrahim manuscript. That this is probably the case appears from the fact that it repeats some of the notes in the Damat Ibrahim manuscript.

---

7 See above, note 5.

II. THE AUTHOR

Both Muẓaffar, the author of the *Naḍrat al-Ighrīḍ*, and his father, Faḍl, are mentioned in Ṣafadī's *Wāfī bi-'l-Wafayāt*, but the information which Ṣafadī offers is rather meagre. Nor did I find much information in other sources. Ibn as Sā'ī confirms a statement in the biography by Ṣafadī that Faḍl became *ḥājib* of the Bāb an-Nūbī [1] in the year 604 [2] and Ḥājjī Khalīfa [3] asserts, without mentioning his source, that Muẓaffar died in 642, the year in which, according to him, the *Naḍra* was composed. Since the two biographies in Ṣafadī's *Wāfī* do not yet exist in print, I reproduce them here in full :

Bodleian, MS Arch. Seld. A 28, fol. 144a :

الفضل بن يحيى بن عبد الله بن جعفر بن زيد بن جعفر بن / محمد بن احمد بن محمد
بن الحسين بن اسحق بن جعفر بن محمد بن على بن الحسين / بن على بن ابى طالب ابو
القاسم بن ابى جعفر بن ابى على العلوى الحسينى / البغدادى ولد بحلب ونشأ
بالموصل وقدم بغداد واستوطنها وصاهر / بيت المعمر [4] النقباء وكان صدرا نبيلا وقورا
اديبا حسن الاخلاق متواضعا / تولى حجابة باب النوبى سنة اربع وست ماية وعاد
الى الكرخ ولزم منزله / الى حين وفاته سنة اربع وعشرين وست ماية.

---

1 For the Bāb an-Nūbī see Le Strange, *Baghdad During the Abbasid Caliphate*, pp. 272 and 274-276.

2 Ibn as-Sā'ī, *al-Jāmi' al-Mukhtaṣar* (ed. Muṣṭafā Jawād), p. 228 : وفى عشية اليوم المذكور (17 Rajab) ولى شرف الدين الفضل بن يحيى العلوى المعروف بابن الموصلى حجبة باب النوبى الشريف وخلع عليه واسكن دار ابن زعلى بدرب فراشا.

The name Ibn al-Mawṣilī shows that the family had close ties with Mosul, a fact which is also borne out by passages in the *Naḍra* (cf. below, p. 32-33).

3 *Kashf aẓ-Ẓunūn*, VI, 353.

4 For the Banū (al-)Mu'ammar see L. Massignon, "Cadis et Naqibs Baghdadiens" in *WZKM*, LI (1948-52), 113.

VIENNA, N F 234[b], fol. 169b, and TUNIS 4850[c] [5], fol. 70a-b :

المظفر بن الفضل بن يحيى ابو على العلوى الحسينى ولد بالموصل ونشأ بها وقدم بغداد وقرأ بها الادب وحفظ اشعار العرب ولم يزل يرتفع فى فضله وحظه الى ان تعدى اقرانه وكان حسن الاخلاق كريم الطباع كبير النفس متواضعا مولده سنة اربع وثمانين وخمسمائة ومن شعره :

كيف [6] يشتاقك قلب * انت فى السوداء منه
انما يشتـاقـك الطرف * الذى قد غبت عنه

ومنه ايضا [7] :

ومنعمة الحجلين يشكو وشاحها * الى القلب ما يشكوه من قلق الوجد
اتتنى وقد نام السمير [8] ولم اكن * على طمع فى الوصل منها ولا الوعد
فبتنا جميعا والعفـاف رقيبـنـا * وكف عـلى كـف وخـد عـلى خـد

قلت شعر متوسط.

Some additional information is supplied by Ḥusaynī himself in the *Naḍra*. On fols. 42a and 229a he quotes traditions on questions of literary theory and criticism and mentions that the traditions were, in the first case, transmitted to him by one ʿAbdarraḥmān al-Wāsiṭī and, in the second case, by one ʿAbdarraḥmān ad-Daqqāq (who may be the same person), and that he studied the texts under this ʿAbdarraḥmān (*bi-qirāʾatī ʿalayhi*) [9]. On fols. 164b, 170a, and 205b he mentions his father as an authority. In view of the fact that Ṣafadī qualifies Ḥusaynī's father as an *adīb*, it could very well be that Ḥusaynī received part of his scholarly instruction from him. The only person, however, whom he explicitly mentions as his teacher (he uses the term *muʾaddibī*) is one Abū Muḥ. b. Abi 'l-Barakāt b. al-Baqqāl al-Muqriʾ al-Muʾaddib. In addition to this, Ḥusaynī refers several

[5] See B. Roy, *Extrait du Catalogue... de la bibliothèque de la Grande Mosquée de Tunis*, p. 38.
[6] Missing in the Vienna MS.
[7] Missing in the Tunis MS.
[8] Both MSS read الشمير.
[9] See below, p. 33-34.

times to a *Risāla 'Alawiyya* of his own composition. He gives no particulars on this *risāla*, but since he mentions it in three places (fols. 128a, 222b, and 227b) in connexion with quotations from the poetry of Mutanabbī, it may well have been a monograph on this poet [10]. Finally we learn from the introduction of the *Naḍra* that the work was dedicated to the last of the Abbasid viziers, Mu'ayyad-addīn b. al-'Alqamī (d. 655) who is praised by Ibn at-Ṭiqṭaqā as an accomplished man of letters, a fine calligrapher, and a bibliophile [11].

The text as a whole shows Ḥusaynī as a rather colourless compilator, whose ability to bring together material from texts of widely different character covering not only literary theory, but also prosody and some episodes of literary history, cannot make up for the fact that he is sorely lacking in accuracy and insight. The apparent popularity of the treatise must therefore be explained by the wealth of quotations and anecdotes it offers rather than by its scholarly or didactic merits. In this respect Ḥusaynī's *Naḍra* closely ressembles Usāma's *Badī' fī Naqd ash-Shi'r* [12] which, however, is much more limited in scope.

---

10 On fol 13a, however, he states that the *Risāla 'Alawiyya* contains a discussion of the term *faṣāḥa*, so that the work could also have had a much wider scope.

11 *Al-Fakhrī* (ed. Ahlwardt), pp. 388-390. In the Introduction Ḥusaynī refers to Ibn al-'Alqamī as مولانا صدر صدور الانام ملك وزراء الشرق والغرب النافذة اوامره فى البعد والقرب مؤيد الدين رضى امير المؤمنين ابى طالب محمد بن أحمد (fol. 2a-b). The words وعددت من زمرة غاشيته وسعدت بالانتهاء الى جملة حاشيته at the end of the treatise (fol. 240b) suggest that Ḥusaynī belonged to Ibn al-'Alqamī's entourage.

12 Ed. Dr. Aḥmad Aḥmad Badawī and Dr. Ḥāmid 'Abdalmajīd (Cairo, 1380/1960).

III. TABLE OF CONTENTS

DEPENDENCE UPON EARLIER TEXTS OF LITERARY CRITICISM

Though I do not intend to offer a survey of the contents of the *Naḍrat al-Ighrīḍ*, but will limit myself to a few passages that are of particular interest, it will be useful to quote at least the titles of the chapters into which the work is divided. An outline of the main sections (*fuṣūl*) is given by Ḥusaynī himself in the Introduction (fols. 4a-5a) [1]. In addition to this, there is at the beginning of the first section (fols. 7a-8a) an outline of the chapters (*abwāb*) which make up this particular section. This second outline qualifies as *alqāb* all terms occurring in the chapter headings from the *Bāb al-Ishāra* onward (including, apparently, the term *naqd* !) [2]. There are slight differences between the titles as they appear in the second outline and in the text itself. I have put such variants between brackets. Moreover, Ḥusaynī sometimes mentions at the beginning of a chapter a synonym of the technical term as it appears in the chapter heading. In such cases I have put a line over the chapter heading (which is always in larger characters) to distinguish it from the synonym which is properly part of the text of the chapter itself.

1b : Introduction.

4a : Outline of the five sections (*fuṣūl*) into which the work is divided.

5a : الفصل الاول فى وصف الشعر واحكامه وبيان احواله واقسامه

8a : النحو

10b : البلاغة

---

1 This outline of *fuṣūl* is quoted in an abbreviated form by Ḥājjī Khalīfa, VI, 353-354.

2 Fol. 7a : واما الشعر فيحتاج الى آلات وفيه القاب / وله صفات ونحن نذكر ذلك مجملا ونشرحه مفصلا / ولا نقصد فيه الترتيب اذ تقديم فصل على فصل غير / مفتقر الى التهذيب. فى الشعر / [fol. 7b] النحو والبلاغة والفصاحة والحقيقة والمجاز / والصنعة والمصنوع واقامة الوزن والقوافى / والالقاب وهى الاشارة ... [fol. 8a] ... والنقد / وغير ذلك مما سنبينه ونوضحه ونعينه ونشرحه على / سبيل الاختصار دون الاكثار ...

13a : الفصاحة

13b : الحقيقة والمجاز

15a : الصنعة والمصنوع

16a : اقامة الوزن

17b : القوافى

19b : الاشارة

21a : باب الكناية وربما سماها قوم التتبيع

24b : باب الموازنة (outline : الموازنة وهى المماثلة)

26b : باب التجنيس

28a : التجنيس المحض

29b : تجنيس اللفظ وربما سموه المطلق

31b : التجنيس المغاير

33b : التجنيس المقارب

35a : تجنيس المعنى

36a : المجنّس المطمع

37a : التجنيس المبدل

38a : المجنّس المختلف

39a : تجنيس الخط ويسمى التصحيف

40a : تجنيس البعض

41a : المجنّس المتمّم

42b : تجنيس القوافى

45b : التجنيس المماثل

46b : باب المطابقة (outline : الطباق)

49a : باب التصدير ويلقبه قوم ردّ اعجاز الكلام على صدوره

49b : باب الالتفات

50b : باب الاستطراد

53a : باب التقسيم

---

3 So also in both the outline and the text of the Vienna manuscript. The Tunis manuscript has تجاهل العارف in the outline, but تجاهل التعارف in the text.

4 From Ḥusaynī's discussion of this term it appears to be a synonym of *tamlīṭ* (see Ibn Rashīq, *ʿUmda* [Cairo, 1325/1907], II, 74 and *Tāj al-ʿArūs*, s.v.), i.e. a poetic contest in which two poets compose alternately a hemistich of the same poem till one of them gives up. As far as I know the term is not commonly used in this sense. The *Tāj al-ʿArūs* (s.v. *m-t-n*) only knows it in the general sense of 'poetic contest' (والماتنة المعارضة فى جدل او خصومة ومنه الماتنة فى الشعر وقد تماتنا ايهما امتن شعرا), and in this sense it is apparently also used in a tradition attributed to Abū ʿAmr b. al-ʿAlāʾ (see *ʿUmda*, I, 135).

112a : الفصل الثانى فيما يجوز للشاعر استعماله وما لا يجوز وما يدرك به صواب القول ويجوز

120a : التضمين

140b : الخزم

142a : الفصل الثالث فى فضله ومنافعه وتاثيره فى القلوب ومواقعه

172b : الفصل الرابع فى كشف ما مدح به وذم بسببه وهل تعاطيه اصلح ام رفضه اوفر وارجح

197a : الفصل الخامس فيما يجب ان يتوخاه الشاعر ويتجنبه ويطرحه ويتطلبه

While introducing his outline of the first section Ḥusaynī informs us that no principle will be observed in the order of the chapters in this section [5]; and in fact the arrangement of the chapters does not, as far I know, correspond to that found in any similar work on literary theory. In spite of this there can be no doubt that Ḥusaynī depends to a considerable extent on earlier authors who wrote on the *balāgha*. This is true particularly of the first and the last sections. The following is a list of these authors as far as they are mentioned by Ḥusaynī himself and of the borrowings I was able to discover :

(*a*) On fols. 34b and 59b Ḥusaynī quotes Ibn al-Muʿtazz, but in both cases it is doubtful whether he had the actual text of Ibn al-Muʿtazz's *Kitāb al-Badīʿ* in front of him. In the first passage he states that the line by Zuhayr :

كأن عينى وقد سال السليل بهم * وجيرة ما هم لو أنهم أمم

which corresponds to p. 28 (no. 98) of the *Kitāb al-Badīʿ* [6] is quoted by Ibn al-Muʿtazz as an example of the *mujannas maḥḍ* (Ḥusaynī himself would consider it no more than a *tajnīs mutaqārib mutashābih*). The term *mujannas maḥḍ*, however, is not used by Ibn al-Muʿtazz who simply quotes the line as an example of the *tajnīs*. In the second passage which corresponds to p. 62 in the *Kitāb al-Badīʿ* he quotes Ibn al-Muʿtazz's term *ta'kīd al-madḥ bimā yushbih adh-dhamm* as a definition of the term *istithnā'* which is the subject of this particular chapter in the *Naḍra*. He then quotes the two verse examples which Ibn al-Muʿtazz gives of the figure *ta'kīd al-madḥ* (*K. al-Badīʿ*, p. 62, nos 232 and 233), without, however, distinguishing between an-Nābigha adh-Dhubyānī and an-Nābigha al-Jaʿdī, as Ibn al-Muʿtazz does [7]. The chapter as a whole shows many points of resem-

---

[5] See above, p. 11 note 2.

[6] Ed. Kratchkovsky (London, 1935).

[7] *Naḍra*, fols. 59b-60a : باب الاستثناء / وقد عبر عنه جماعة فكان اقرب اقوالهم الى القلب ما ذكره / عبد الله بن المعتز فانه قال الاستثناء فى الشعر / [60a] تاكيد مدح بما يشبه الذم فمن ذلك / قول النابغة /

ولا عيب فيهم غير ان سيوفهم * بهن فلول من قراع الكتائب/

blance with the *istithnā'* chapter in the *Ḥilyat al-Muḥāḍara* of Ḥātimī, even though in Ḥātimī's chapter the term *ta'kīd al-madḥ bimā yushbih adh-dhamm* is not attributed to Ibn al-Mu'tazz [8]. The only passage in the *Naḍra* that closely corresponds to the *Kitāb al-Badī'* is the beginning of the *iltifāt* chapter, where the definition and the first example are identical [9]. In this last passage, however, the name of Ibn al-Mu'tazz is not mentioned and other parts of the chapter agree with the *iltifāt* chapter in the *Ḥilyat al-Muḥāḍara*, so that it is again more likely that Ḥusaynī took the definition and the example from that author [10]. The same is probably the case with another Ibn al-Mu'tazz quotation which was not taken from the *Kitāb al-Badī'* and will be discussed later [11].
Finally there is a parallel between Ḥusaynī's criticism of a line by A'shā (fol. 100a-b) and Ibn al-Mu'tazz's criticism of the same line as quoted in Marzubānī's *Kitāb al-Muwashshaḥ* [12]. The passage occurs in the *Naḍra* in the paragraph on the ninth form (*wajh*) of reprehensible *sariqa*. I quote it here in full :

...وقال الاعشى /

فرميت غفلة عينه عن شاته * فاصبت حبّة قلبه وطحالها /

[100b] اما ذكر القلب والفؤاد والكبد فلا ريب انه يتردد كثيرا / فى الشعر عند ذكر الهوى والمحبة والشوق وما يجده المغرم / فى هذه الاعضاء من الالم والحرارة والكرب

واما النحويون فالاستثناء فى الكلام عندهم استخراج / بعض من كل فى حكم شامل بمعنى آلا / وقال ايضا /

فتى كملت اخلاقه غير انه * جواد فما يبقى من المال باقيا / ... الخ

8 Cf. below, p. 30 and note 46.

9 *Naḍra*, fols. 49b-50a : باب الالتفات/ [50a] وهو انصراف عن مخاطبة الى اخبار وعن اخبار الى مخاطبة / وهو من بديع البديع قال جرير /

متى كان الخيام بذى طلوح * سقيت الغيث ايتها الخيام /
اتذكر يوم تصقل عارضيها * بعود بشامة سقى البشام /

ويروى /

اتنسى اذ توعّدنا سليمى * بعود بشامة سقى البشام /

(cf. Ibn al-Mu'tazz, *K. al-Badī'*, p. 58-59).

10 See below, p. 21.

11 See below, p. 31. It is possible that some further parallels could be established by comparing verse examples in the *Naḍra* and the *K. al-Badī'*, but one has to bear in mind that very often the same examples appear in every text dealing with literary theory, which deprives such parallels of much of their significance.

12 Printed in Cairo in 1343 from a copy made by Shinqīṭī of the unique Istanbul manuscript.

واما الطحال / فما راينا احدا استعمل ذكره فى هذه الاحوال اذ لا صنع له / فيها

ولا هو مما ينسب الى حركة فى حزن او عشق ولا الى / سكون عند فرح او ظفر

ففساد ذكر الطحال ظاهر فى / هذه الحال.

The resemblance between this passage and the Ibn al-Muʿtazz quotation in the *Kitāb al-Muwashshaḥ* (p. 56) is clear. Again however the name of Ibn al-Muʿtazz is not mentioned in the *Naḍra* and there is no way of knowing for certain where Ḥusaynī found the passage [13].

(*b*) Ḥusaynī quotes on fol. 34b one Ibn Qudāma and on fol. 58b one Jaʿfar b. Qudāma. On fols. 218a-219a, 219b, 220a-222a, 223a, 225a-b, and 226a we find passages which are clearly derived from the *Naqd ash-Shiʿr* of Qudāma b. Jaʿfar [14]. These passages deal with the *tanāquḍ* (corresponding in part to *Naqd*, pp. 128-130), the *tathlīm* (corresponding in part to *Naqd*, p. 136-137), the *taghyīr* (corresponding in part to *Naqd*, p. 138), the *tadhnīb* (corresponding to *Naqd*, p. 137-138), the *ikhlāl* (corresponding in part to *Naqd*, p. 134-135), the *ziyāda* (corresponding to *Naqd*, p. 136 : *ʿaks al-ʿayb al-mutaqaddim*), the *fasād at-tafsīr* (corresponding in part to *Naqd*, p. 122-123), the *takalluf al-qawāfī wa-ʾstidʿāʾuhā* (corresponding in part to *Naqd*, p. 140-141), a verse example corresponding to nº 685 (p. 142) in the last chapter of the *Naqd* which has no special title, but is independent of the preceding chapter on the *istidʿāʾ al-qawāfī* (Ḥusaynī's commentary is similar to Qudāma's), two verse examples corresponding to nºs 653 and 654 (p. 133-134) of the chapter on the *mukhālafat al-ʿurf* in the *Naqd* (part of Ḥusaynī's commentary is similar to Qudāma's), and three examples corresponding to nºs 537, 541, and 545 (p. 102) of the chapter on the *waḥshī* in the *Naqd* which Ḥusaynī, however, discusses in a chapter on ugly rhymes.

The order of the chapters in the *Naḍra* does not correspond to that in the *Naqd*. Nor do Ḥusaynī's terminology, his definitions, and the commentaries on the examples always agree with Qudāma's. This and the fact that Ḥusaynī does

---

13 It is tempting to suggest that Ḥusaynī copied the passage from the Istanbul manuscript of the *Muwashshaḥ* mentioned in the preceding note. This manuscript was written in 637 and belonged to Ibn al-ʿAlqamī (see Bonebakker, *The Kitāb Naqd al-Šiʿr of Qudāma b. Ǧaʿfar*, Introduction, p. 63-64) to whose entourage Ḥusaynī belonged. There are however some small differences between the two texts and, as I explained above, it is very difficult to establish convincing parallels between works like the *Muwashshaḥ* (which consists entirely of short fragments of early criticism of a type found in many other *adab* works) and any later work on literary theory. For a similar case see below, p. 20. For similar criticism by older philologists of the same line by Aʿshā see *Muwashshaḥ*, p. 55-56; *Aghānī*[1] (Cairo, 1258), IX, 41-42 (= *idem*[2] [Cairo, 1371/1952], X, 81-82). Ḥātimī's criticism of this line is different from that of Ibn al-Muʿtazz (see Ibn Rashīq, *ʿUmda*, II, 57-58).

14 Ed. Bonebakker, *The Kitāb Naqd al-Šiʿr of Qudāma b. Ǧaʿfar al-Kātib al-Baġdādī* (Leiden, 1956).

not mention Qudāma in these passages makes it likely that he had no first-hand knowledge of the *Naqd*, or used a different work by the same author or, which is more likely, copied out quotations of which he did not know the origin. The problem is further complicated by the two quotations from Ibn Qudāma and Ja'far b. Qudāma. In the first quotation Ḥusaynī states that Ibn Qudāma agrees with Ibn al-Mu'tazz in classifying the line by Zuhayr (corresponding to nº 505 on p. 93 of the *Naqd*) as a *mujannas maḥḍ* [15]. In the second quotation one 'Alī b. al-Ḥusayn al-Qurashī asks Ja'far b. Qudāma whom he considers one of the outstanding experts on poetry to explain the term *muqābala* to him. Ja'far then quotes his father on the subject. The passage shows close resemblance to part of the corresponding chapter in the *Naqd* (p. 72-73), but, as will be shown later, the whole *muqābala* chapter in the *Naḍra* was borrowed from a work by Ḥātimī, either his *Ḥilyat al-Muḥāḍara* or some other work from which Ḥusaynī drew directly or through quotations [16]. In the *Ḥilya* the same passage is introduced in the following way :

قال ابو على (= الحاتمى) اخبرنى على بن الحسن (or : الحسين) القرشى قال سألت
قدامة عن المقابلة فقال هو ان يضع...

I am unable to offer a wholly satisfactory solution to the difficult questions raised by this passage and the passage on fol. 34b. What seems certain is that we have to read على بن الحسين القرشى and not على بن الحسن القرشى in the *Ḥilya* manuscript, and that this 'Alī b. al-Ḥusayn al-Qurashī is identical with Abu 'l-Faraj 'Alī b. al-Ḥusayn al-Qurashī al-Iṣfahānī, the author of the *Kitāb al-Aghānī*. For in other *isnāds* Ḥātimī quotes the name as Abu 'l-Faraj 'Alī b. al-Ḥusayn al-Qurashī [17]. I have given elsewhere my reasons for believing that the Ja'far b. Qudāma b. Ziyād mentioned in the *Ta'rīkh Baghdād* is the father of Qudāma b. Ja'far [18]. This Ja'far b. Qudāma, as we learn from the *Ta'rīkh Baghdād*, was quoted as an authority by Abu 'l-Faraj al-Iṣfahānī. Nothing, therefore, would seem more obvious than to assume that the text of the note on the *mu-*

---

15 See above, p. 12.

16 See below, p. 28-29.

17 Cf. also Khafājī, *Sirr al-Faṣāḥa* (ed. 'Abdalmuta'āl aṣ-Ṣa'īdī), p. 234. Khafājī quoting from a chapter by Ḥātimī on the *muṭābaqa* (cf. *Ḥilya*, MS Fez 2934, fol 6a) gives the name as Abu 'l-Faraj 'Alī b. al-Ḥusayn al-Iṣfahānī. See also below, p. 18.

18 See Bonebakker, *The Kitāb Naqd al-Ši'r*, Introduction, pp. 3-5. To the texts quoted there, Marzubānī, *Muwashshaḥ*, p. 378 should be added. In this passage one Abū Qudāma is mentioned as a man who composed bad verse. It may well be that this Abū Qudāma and the person Ibn an-Nadīm had in mind when he qualified Qudāma's father as an ignoramus, are identical, but have nothing to do with the father of the author of the *Naqd*.

qābala as it appears in the *Naḍra* is correct and that the *Ḥilya* text as we have it in the MS 2934 of the Qarawiyyīn Mosque in Fez (the MS 590 of the same text is incomplete and does not give the passage) mistakenly reads Qudāma for Ja'far b. Qudāma and omits the سألت ابى عنها فقال of the *Naḍra*. This would mean that the discussion of the *muqābala* as we have it in the *Naqd* goes back to Qudāma's grandfather which, knowing that some of the figures of speech were discussed before Ibn al-Mu'tazz's time, would not be altogether impossible. Still I believe that it is not necessary to accept this as the only, or even the most likely, conclusion. Ḥusaynī is by no means a very knowledgeable author. The resemblance of the text on fols. 58b-59a in the *Naḍra* and on fol. 8a of the *Ḥilya* to the chapter in the *Naqd* is so striking that it is hard to believe that it could go back to anyone but Qudāma, the author of the *Naqd*. Assuming that the سألت ابى عنها فقال belongs to the original text, but has been skipped over by the scribe of the *Ḥilya* manuscript (the occurrence within a short distance of each other of two *qāla*s makes this very easy) one could imagine that Ḥusaynī (or the author of the text from which he is quoting) was not aware of the fact that Qudāma's father had a reputation as an authority on poetry and only knew of Qudāma, the son and author of the *Naqd ash-Shi'r*. He might well have decided that Qudāma b. Ja'far was only a misreading for Ja'far b. Qudāma and changed the text accordingly. It is quite possible that Abu 'l-Faraj al-Iṣfahānī knew both Ja'far b. Qudāma, the father, and Qudāma b. Ja'far, the son, but it is more difficult to believe that he knew Ja'far b. Qudāma b. Ziyād, Qudāma b. Ja'far, and a grandson by the name of Ja'far b. Qudāma. Elsewhere in the same manuscript of the *Ḥilya* (fol. 7a) Abu 'l-Faraj 'Alī b. al-Ḥusayn al-I[ṣ]bahānī (here one has the *nisba* Iṣbahānī instead of Qurashī!) asks a scholar whose name has become partly illegible, but who may very well be Qudāma (the MS 590 of the *Ḥilya* again does not have the passage) what is the best example of the *tajnīs* quoted in his book. In reply to Iṣfahānī's question this scholar then quotes a line by an unnamed poet of the tribe of 'Abs which occurs on p. 95 (n° 513) of the *Naqd*. If one accepts this theory one would have to assume that Ḥusaynī changed Qudāma into Ibn Qudāma on fol. 34b to bring this earlier quotation in line with the quotation on fol. 58b. In this connexion it is also interesting to note that on fol. 5b of the *Ḥilya* manuscript in the chapter on *al-waḥy wa-'l-ishāra* we find commentaries on a line by an unnamed Jāhilī poet and on a line by 'Abdarraḥmān b. 'Alī b. 'Alqama b. 'Abada which resemble very closely Qudāma's remarks on these same lines in his *tamthīl* chapter in the *Naqd* (n°s 495 and 497 on p. 91-92). In the *Ḥilya* these commentaries, which go back to Isḥāq al-Mawṣilī, are quoted on the authority of Isḥāq's son Ḥammād [19].

---

[19] He transmitted the *Kitāb al-Aghānī* of his father and transmitted, together with his father, from Abū 'Ubayda and Aṣma'ī. See R. Sellheim, *Die Gelehrtenbiographien des Abū 'Ubaydallāh al-Marzubānī* (Bibliotheca Islamica 23a), p. 322 and al-Khaṭīb al-Baghdādī, *Ta'rīkh Baghdād*, VIII, 159 (n° 4263). See also the numerous *isnāds* that contain the name of Ḥammād in Marzubānī's *Muwashshaḥ*.

The same Ḥammād b. Isḥāq was, according to the *Ta'rīkh Baghdād*, one of the teachers of Jaʿfar b. Qudāma b. Ziyād. The passage is interesting enough to be quoted here :

اخبرنا ابو على[20] قال اخبرنى على بن هرون / قال اخبرنى ابى هرون بن على عن حماد بن اسحق قال قلت لابى اسحق بن ابرهيم اسمعك تكرر ذكر[21] / الاشارة فى الشعر وتشير الى انها من محاسنه فما هى قال قول الشاعر /

اوردته وصدور العيس مسنفة * والليل[22] بالكوكب الدرّىّ منحور

وقول الاخر /

جعلنا السيف بين الجيد منه * وبين سواد لحيته عذارا[23] /

ثم قال الا ترى الى قوله اوردته وصدور العيس مسنفة وقد اشار الى الفجر اشارة[24] ظريفة بغير لفظه / قال ثم قال لى هذا هو[25] الوحى ومثاله قول / جاهلى /

جعلت يدىّ وشاحا له * وبعض الفوارس لا يعتنق /

قال فقوله جعلت يدىّ وشاحا له اشارة بديعة[26] بغير لفظ الاعتناق وهى دالة عليه[27] /

---

20 = Ḥātimī (cf. Ibn Rashīq, *ʿUmda*, I, 206). Ḥātimī frequently uses the formulas *akhbaranā* and *akhbarakum* in front of his own name.

21 Missing in the MS 590, fol. 8b.

22 My friend Mr. Kamal Abu Deeb of Trinity College, Oxford, points out to me that the reading *wa-'l-laylu* for *wa-'ṣ-ṣubḥu* in this quotation is unusual and I have in fact not been able to find it elsewhere. In the context of this tradition it is more suitable than *wa-'ṣ-ṣubḥu* and should perhaps not be rejected as a mere copyist's error.

23 Quoted in *ʿUmda*, I, 206 from Ḥātimī.

24 The MS 590, fol. 8b reads استعارة.

25 Missing in the MS 590.

26 So in the MS 590, fol. 8b. Illegible in the MS 2934.

27 Immediately following this tradition the *Ḥilya* (MS 2934, fol. 5b; MS 590, fols. 8b-9a) has another tradition on Qudāma (this time the name is clearly legible). It goes back to one ʿĪsā b. ʿAbdalʿazīz aṭ-Ṭāhirī who meets Qudāma and obtains from him a definition of the *ishāra* and two examples corresponding to *Naqd*, nº 471 (p. 86) and nº 474 (p. 87).

All this evidence, I believe, shows that one can at least make a case for limiting this particular tradition of studies on literary theory to two scholars, Qudāma b. Ja'far, author of the *Naqd ash-Shi'r*, and his father, Ja'far b. Qudāma b. Ziyād. Muṭarrizī (d. 610), the one author who mentions that there was some uncertainty over the authorship of the *Naqd ash-Shi'r*, mentions Qudāma's father as the only alternative [28]. Unless some further evidence is discovered there may not be sufficient reason to bring Qudāma's grandfather, Ziyād, or a son of Qudāma by the name of Ja'far into the picture [29].

(*c*) Ḥusaynī was well acquainted with the work of Ibn Ṭabāṭabā al-'Alawī (d. 322), though he mentions this author only in two places (fols. 199b and 231b) and does not give the title of his only extant work on rhetoric, the *'Iyār ash-Shi'r* [30]. Ḥusaynī's dependence on his early predecessor is demonstrated by passages on fols. 197b (cf. *'Iyār*, p. 4), 197b-198a (cf. *'Iyār*, p. 5), 198a (cf. *'Iyār*, p. 9-10), 198b (cf. *'Iyār*, p. 10), 198b-199a (cf. *'Iyār*, p. 10), 199a (cf. *'Iyār*, p. 124), 199a-b (cf. *'Iyār*, p. 126), and 199b (cf. *'Iyār*, p. 124-125). (There may be other passages which escaped my attention.) It is possible, however, that Ḥusaynī knew Ibn Ṭabāṭabā only from quotations and that these quotations were based on a work related to, but not identical with, the *'Iyār ash-Shi'r*. This would seem to be the case with a passage on fols. 231a-232a. This passage shows some affinity with the opening lines of the chapter on the *ta'līf ash-shi'r* on p. 124 of the *'Iyār* and quotes the example on p. 125, but resembles more closely a quotation on p. 237 of Marzubānī's *Muwashshaḥ*, where this example immediately follows the remarks of the opening lines of the *'Iyār* chapter. I reproduce here the passage from the *Naḍra* :

وينبغى للشاعر ان يوفق بين التشبيه والمشبه / به ويراعى ذلك بحيث لا ياتى
الكلام متنافرا والمعانى متباعدة / فانه اذا انعم النظر فى تاليف شعره وتنسيق ابياته
ووقف / على حسن تجاورها او قبحه فلأم بينها ونظم معانيها ووصل /[231b] الكلام
فيها كان مجيدا وكان مع الشعراء المجيدين معدودا / الا ترى ابن هرمة وقوله /

---

[28] See Bonebakker, *The Kitāb Naqd al-Ši'r*, Introduction, p. 4.

[29] An abstract of the *Naqd ash-Shi'r* in the Bibliothèque des Lettres in Tunis (MS 390 R, fols. 21a-27b) gives the name of the author as Abū Ja'far Qudāma b. Ja'far b. Qudāma al-Baghdādī. This abstract is in the handwriting of one Ḥammūda b. Muḥ. an-Nurī al-Būbakrī. A manuscript in the Maktaba Waṭaniyya in Tunis (nº 1344) of the complete text of the *Naqd* in the handwriting of the same Ḥammūda b. Muḥ. an-Nūrī gives only Qudāma b. Ja'far al-Baghdādī. The abstract is undated, but the manuscript of the complete text carries the date 1294. The two manuscripts were unknown to me at the time I was preparing my edition of the *Naqd*.

[30] Ed. Dr. Ṭāhā al-Ḥājirī and Dr. Muḥ. Zaghlūl Salām (Cairo, 1956).

وانى وتركى ندى الاكرمين * وقدحى بكفّى زنادا شحاحا /

كتاركة بيضها بالعراء * وملبسة بيض اخرى جناحا /

والفرزدق وقوله /

وانك اذ تهجو تميما وترتشى * سرابيل قيس او سحوق العمائم /

كمهريق ماء الفلاة وغرّه * سراب اذاعته رياح السمائم /

قال ابن طباطبا العلوى / لو ان ثانى بيتى ابن هرمة عوض عن ثانى بيتى الفرزدق وثانى / بيتى الفرزدق عوض عن ثانى بيتى ابن هرمة لصح التشبيه / لهما واتسقت معانى شعريهما والا فالتشبيه فى الشعرين / [232a] غير واقع موقعه وهذا نقد من ابن طباطبا فى اعلى / درجات الحسن والادراك.

That Ibn Ṭabāṭabā could very well have borrowed the passage from Marzubānī appears from the Ibn al-Muʿtazz quotation mentioned earlier and from an *isnād* on fol. 229a which contains the name of Marzubānī [31]. Moreover, Marzubānī's writings on literary criticism were not limited to the *Muwashshaḥ* (which is rather a collection of early traditions, not an original work), so that the other passages in the *Naḍra* that show Ḥusaynī's dependence on Ibn Ṭabāṭabā may very well have reached him through some other work by the same author.

(*d*) Even more than from Ibn al-Muʿtazz, Qudāma, and Ibn Ṭabāṭabā, Ḥusaynī seems to have borrowed from Ḥātimī (d. 388). I established this by comparing several of Ḥusaynī's chapters on figures of speech with corresponding chapters in the unedited *Ḥilyat al-Muḥāḍara* by Ḥātimī. The dependence of Ḥusaynī on Ḥātimī is, I believe, beyond doubt in the chapters on the *taṣdīr*, the *tashīm*, and the *muqābala*. Ḥusaynī actually quotes Ḥātimī by name in his chapter on the *tardīd*. In the case of the chapters on the *ishāra*, the *muṭābaqa*, the *iltifāt*, the *istiṭrād*, the *taqsīm*, the *istithnā'*, the *īghāl*, the *istiʿāra*, the *tashbīh*, the *ḥashw*, and the *takhalluṣ*, it appears very likely that he took part or all of each chapter from his predecessor. As in the case of the three other authors, it is possible that Ḥusaynī did not borrow directly from Ḥātimī, but only knew this author from

31 See below, p. 33.

quotations; or that he used a work different from the *Ḥilya* by the same author, for instance the *Kitāb al-Ḥālī wa-'l-'Āṭil* [32]. This would explain many of the differences that exist between chapters in the *Naḍra* and corresponding chapters in the *Ḥilya*.

The four chapters in which the dependence of Ḥusaynī on Ḥātimī appears indisputable are interesting enough to be quoted here in full :

Naḍra, fol. 49a-b :

باب التصدير / ويلقبه قوم ردّ اعجاز الكلام على صدوره وهو ان يبتدئ / الشاعر بكلمة فى البيت ثم يعيدها فى عجزه او نصفه ثم يردّها / فى النصف الاخير واذا نظم الشعر على هذه الصنعة تيسر / استخراج قوافيه قبل ان تطرق اسماع مستمعيه / قال الاصمعى من حسن التصدير قول عامر بن الطفيل وكذى / [49b] قال جماعة من نقاد الشعر /

فكنت سناما فى فزارة تامكا * وفى كل حىّ ذروة وسنام /

وقال قوم بل من جيد التصدير قول جرير /

سقى الرمل جون مستهلّ ربابه * وما ذاك الا حبّ من حلّ بالرمل /

وقال اخرون بل قول الاول من حسن التصدير /

سريع الى ابن العمّ يشتم عرضه * وليس الى داعى الندى بسريع /

وقال اناس قول ابن احمر من جيد ما قيل فى التصدير وهو /

تغمرت منها بعد ما نفد الصبى * ولم يرو من ذى حاجة من تغمرا /

والتغمر الشرب القليل وقال الفرزدق /

اصدر همومك لا يقتلك واردها * فكل واردة يوما لها صدر /

---

[32] See however Ibn Abi 'l-Iṣba', *Badī' al-Qur'ān* (ed. Ḥifnī Muḥ. Sharaf), text, p. 4. Ibn Abi 'l-Iṣba' never met anybody who had seen a copy of the *Kitāb al-Ḥālī* and only found it mentioned in the *Badī'* of Usāma b. Munqidh (cf. p. 8 of the edition mentioned above, p. 10, note 12).

Ḥātimī, *Ḥilyat al-Muḥāḍara* (MS Fez, Qarawiyyīn 2934), fol. 10a :

احسن ما قيل فى التصدير / قال ابو على هو ان يبدأ الشاعر بكلمة فى البيت
ثم [يعيد]ها[33] فى ع[جزه] / او فى النصف منه ثم يرددها فى النصف الاخير
فاذا نظم الشعر على [هذه الصنعة] تهيأ / [است]خراج قوافيه قبل ان تطرق
اسماع مستمعيه قال نقاد الشعر احسن ما قيل فى ذلك قول / [عامر بن] الطفيل :

وكنت سناما فى فزارة تامكا * وفى كل حى ذروة وسنام /

[قا]ل اخرون بل قول جرير /

سقى الرمل جون مستهل ربابـه * وما ذاك الا حب من حل بالرمل /

[و]قال اخرون بل قول الاخر /

سريع الى ابن العم يشتم عرضه * وليس الى داعى الندى بسريع /

[قا]ل ابو على وانا اقول بل قول ابن احمر /

تغمرت منها بعد ما نفد الصبا * ولم يرو من ذى حاجة من تغمرا /

Naḍra, fol. 54b, 55a-b :

باب التسهيم / سئل جماعة ممن يتعاطى علم البديع ونقد الشعر الصنيع عن /
التسهيم فما منهم من اجاب بجواب التفهيم ولم يحصل / من اشاراتهم اليه ونصوصهم
عليه سوى ان المسهّم هو الذى / يسبق السامع الى قوافيه قبل ان ينتهى اليها راويه /

33 The words in brackets are partly or wholly illegible in my microfilm of the MS 2934 (the MS 590 does not have the four chapters). The readings suggested here are supported by Sharīshī's commentary on the *Maqāmāt* of Ḥarīrī (ed. Muḥ. ʿAbdalmunʿim Khafājī, II, 233) which quotes Ḥātimī and contains some chapters on rhetoric that were undoubtedly taken from this author.

(here follows a passage in which Ḥusaynī argues against the use of *tashīm* as a term for this figure. The text continues on fol. 55a).

قال الاخفش ومن ابرع ما قيل فى التسهيم / ما قالته الجنوب اخت عمرو ذى الكلب /

فاقسمت يا عمرو لو نبّهاك * اذن نبّها منك داء عضالا /

اذن نبّها ليث عرّيسة * مفيتا مفيدا نفوسا ومالا /

وخرق تجاوزت مجهوله * بخرقاء حرف تشكّى الكلالا /

فكنت النهار بها [sic] شمسه * وكنت دجى الليل فيها [sic] الهلالا /

[55b] ثم قال انظر الى ديباجة هذا الكلام ما اصفاها والى تقسيماته / ما اوفاها

وانظر الى قولها مفيتا مفيدا والى وصفها اياه فى / النهار بالشمس وفى الليل بالهلال

تجد البعيد المطمع الممتنع / وفى هذه البلغة اليسيرة من هذا الباب كفاية ان شاء الله /

Ḥilya, fol. 8b :

[احسن] ما قيل فى التسهيم / [قال ابو على (؟)] [سأ]لت [34] على بن هرون [و]ما

---

[34] The passages between brackets have been taken from Muḥ. b. Aḥmad al-Gharnāṭī, *Raf' al-Ḥujub al-Mastūra fī Maḥāsin al-Maqṣūra* (Cairo, 1344), I, 29, which quotes a definition of the *tashīm* by Ḥātimi and the poem by Janūb. The text there continues as follows: وقد نقل ابن وكيع هذا الكلام الذى يسند الى على بن هارون ثم قال هذا لقب غير دال على المعنى لفظه وارى الملقب انما قصد الاغراب. The passage in which Ḥusaynī argues against the use of the term *tashīm* begins: قلت ليس هذا اللقب دالا على هذا المعنى فان كان الملقب قصد الاغراب به فقد ابعد المرمى وزل عن النهج الاقوم. In the same paragraph he mentions the term *muṭmi'* which, according to Ibn Rashīq (*'Umda*, II, 26), was used by Ibn Wakī' as an acceptable alternative to *tashīm*. This suggests that Ḥusaynī knew a chapter by Ibn Wakī' on this figure. A further indication that Ḥusaynī depended on Ibn Wakī' is the fact that there is considerable agreement between the titles of the twenty *sariqa* chapters in the *Naḍra* (see above, p. 13; this section of the work is of little interest and I did not quote these titles) and those quoted from the *Munṣif* of Ibn Wakī' in Sharīshī's commentary on the *Maqāmāt* (II, 205-208). I have not found any indication, however, that any of the three authors who quote Ḥātimī: Sharīshī, Gharnāṭī, or Ḥusaynī, knew Ḥātimī through this Ibn Wakī'. Ibn Wakī' (d. 393) was a contemporary of Ḥātimī. He lived in Egypt though his family came originally from Baghdad (see Ibn Khallikān [ed. Wüstenfeld], nº 170 and Brockelmann, *GAL*, G I, 92; S I, 147). It is possible that he did not know Ḥātimī and received the 'Alī b. Hārūn tradition through another channel.

رايت اعلم بصناعة الشعر منه عن [التسهيم] / فقال هذا لقب اخترعناه نحن قلت فما كيفيته فاجابنى بجواب لم يبرزه فى عبارة صحيح[ة الا] / [ان مفهومه ان ص]فة الشعر المسهم ان يسبق المستمع الى قوافيه قبل ان ينتهى اليها راويه / [حتى لو سمع السامع][35] الشطر الاول استخرج الشطر الاخير من قبل ان يسمعه قال واحسن ما / قيل فى ذلك قول [جنوب] اخت عمرو ذى الكلب ترثى اخاها عمرا /

فاقسمت يا عمرو لو نبهاك * اذن نبها منك داء عضالا /
اذا بها [sic] ليث عريسة * مفيتا مفيدا نفوسا ومالا /
وخرق تجاوزت مجهوله * بوجناء خرق [sic] تشكى الكلالا /
فكنت النهار به شمسه * وكنت دجى الليل فيه الهلالا /

قال ابو على فانظر الى ديباجة هذا الكلام ما اصفاها والى تقسيماته ما اوفاها وانظر / الى قولها مفيدا مفيتا [sic] ووصفها اياه بالشمس فى النهار والهلال فى الليل تجد المطمع الممتنع القريب / البعيد.

Naḍra, fol. 57b, 58a-b. :

باب الترديد / وهو ان يعلق الشاعر لفظة فى البيت بمعنى ثم يرددها / فيه بعينها ويعلقها بمعنى أاخر واجمع اهل النقد ان / ابا حيّة النميرى سبق الى هذا الاحسان جميع من تقدمه / وتاخر عنه بقوله /

الا حيّ من اجل الحبيب المغانيا * لبسن البلى مما لبسن اللياليا /
اذا ما تقاضى المرء يوم وليلة * تقاضاه شىء لا يملّ التقاضيا /

[58a] ابتدأ فى المصراع الاول فاحسن الابتداء وردد فى المصراع / الثانى فاحسن الترديد وقال ابو تمام الطائى لا اعرف / احدا احسن صنعة فى الترديد من قول زهير / وهو /

35 The first three words also in Sharīshī, II, 231, who quotes part of the chapter.

من يلق يوما على علّاته هرما * يلق السماحة منه والندى خلقا /

ويروى ان تلق وتلق السماحة قال الاصمعى هذا امدح بيت / قالته العرب وقال ابو على الحاتمى لقد احسن / ابو نواس فى الترديد بقوله /

صفراء لا تنزل الاحزان ساحتها * لو مسّها حجر مسّته سرّاء /

وقال ايضا /

ظن بى من قد كلفت به * فهو يجفونى على الظنن /

[58b] قال الحاتمى ولقد اجاد على بن جبلة مع تاخر زمانه فى صفة / فرس حيث يقول /

مضطرب يرتجّ من اقطاره * كالماء جالت فيه ريح فاضطرب /

اذا تظنّينا به صدقنا * وان تظنّى فوته العير كذب /

والترديد فى اشعار المتاخرين كثير ولكن لم نصرف اليه / همة ففيما اتينا به من المثال كفاية.

Ḥilya, fol. 9a :

احسن ما قيل فى الترد[يد][36] / [ه]و تعليق الشاعر لفظة فى البيت بمعنى [ثم ير]ددها فيه بعينها ويعلقها بمعنى اخر / [واكثر ما] يرد هذا للمحدثين لاكنى ساذكر(؟) احسن ما فى معنا[ه لمتق]دم (؟) قال ابو على وجد[تهم(؟)] / [اجمعوا ان] ابا حية النميرى سبق الى الاحسان جميع من تقدمه [وتاخر ع]نه فى [قوله] /

الا حى من اجل الحبيب المغانيا * لبسن البلى مما لبسن اللياليا /

اذا ما تقاضى المرء يوم وليلة * تقاضاه شىء لا يمل التقاضيا /

[ابتد]ع (؟) بالمصراع الاول فاحسن الابتداء وردد فى المصراع الثانى فاحسن

[36] The words in brackets are again readings suggested by Sharīshī's commentary on the *Maqamāt* (II, 232), except those followed by a question mark.

الترد[يد ...] / الثانى (؟) [مـ]ـمّا (؟) [37] ليس لاحد مثله انا عبد الله بن جعفر بن درستويه قال اخبرنى على [.....] / [.....] [38] عن حبيب [39] لا اعلم احدا احسن فى صناعة الترديد من زهير فى قوله /

من يلق يوما على علاته هرما * يلقى [sic] السماحة منه والندى خلقا /

قال ابو على وقد احسن الخليع الباهلى فى ترديده بقوله /

لقد ملأت عينى بغرّ محاسن * ملأن فؤادى لوعة وهموما /

واحسن ابو نواس فى قوله :

صفراء لا تنزل الاحزان ساحتها * لو مسها حجر مسته سراء /

وعلى بن جبلة على تاخر زمانه فى قوله يصف فرسا /

مضطرب يرتج من اقطاره * كالماء جالت به ريح فاضطرب /

اذا تظنينا به صدقنا * وان تظنى فوته العير كذب /

لا يبلغ الجهد به راكبه * وتبلغ الريح به حيث احب /

Naḍra, 58b, 59a-b :

باب المقابلة / قال على بن الحسين القرشى سألت جعفر بن قدامة الكاتب / وكان من جهابذة الشعر عن المقابلة فقال سألت ابى عنها / فقال هو ان يضع الشاعر

---

37 Read with Sharīshī : ابتدأ بالمصراع الاول فاحسن الابتداء وردد فى المصراع الثانى فاحسن الترديد ثم ابتدع فى البيت الثانى ما...

38 Perhaps [ال]كسورى which might be a misreading for الكسروى. One could suggest على بن مهدى /الكسروى. The poet and scholar ʿAlī b. Mahdī al-Kisrawī died between 283 and 289, see Marzubānī, *Muʿjam ash-Shuʿarāʾ* (Cairo, 1354), p. 292; Yāqūt, *Irshād*, V, 427-432; Suyūṭī, *Bughya*, p. 356. That he was interested in Abū Tammām appears from another quotation in the *Ḥilya* (MS 2934, fol. 67a, with the same *isnād*) and from Marzubānī, *Muwashshaḥ*, pp. 321, 327, and 329.

39 Ḥabīb b. Aws aṭ-Ṭāʾī Abū Tammām.

معانى يعتمد التوفيق بين بعضها / وبعض او المخالفة فياتى بالموافق مع ما يوافقه وفى المخالف /[59a] بما يخالفه على الصحة او يشترط شروطا ويعدد احوالا فى احد / المعنيين فيجب ان ياتى فيما يوافقه بمثل الذى شرط [و]فيما يخالفه / باضداد ذلك قال فقلت له فانشدنى احسن ما قيل فيه فقال / لا اعرف احسن من قول الاول /

ايا عجبا كيف اتفقنا فناصح * وفىّ ومطوىّ على الغلّ غادر /

فجعل بازاء ناصح مطويّا على الغلّ وبازاء وفىّ غادرا قال وقول / الطرماح بن جهم [sic] الطائى فى ذلك حسن ايضا وهو /

اسرناهم وانعمنا عليهم * واسقينا دماهم الترابا /

فما صبروا لبأس عند حرب * ولا ادّوا بحسن يد ثوابا /

يقول لما سقينا التراب دماهم لم يكن / لهم صبر على ما نزل بهم منا لفشلهم وضعف نفوسهم ولما / [59b] انعمنا عليهم واحسنا اليهم لم يجازوا بالثناء علينا فجعل بازاء / ان سقوا دماهم التراب وقاتلوهم ان يصبروا وبازاء ان / انعموا عليهم ان يثنوا وقال هذه المقابلة / وقال على بن هرون كان يحيى بن على يزعم ان احسن ما قيل فى / المقابلة قول النابغة /

فتى تمّ فيه ما يسرّ صديقه * على ان فيه ما يسوء المعاديا [40] /

فجعل بازاء السرور الاساأة وبازاء الصديق المعادى / وهذه نغبة فى هذا الباب كافية.

Ḥilya, fol. 8a-b :

احسن ما ورد فى المقابلة / قال ابو على اخبرنى على بن الحسن (or : الحسين) القرشى قال سألت قدامة عن المقابلة فقال هو ان / يضع الشاعر المعانى يعتمد التوفيق

[40] In the margin : الاعاديا خ.

بين بعضها وبعض والمخالفة [sic] فياتى فى المخالف بما يخالف / وفى الموافق بما يوافق على الصحة او يشترط شرطا [sic] ويقدر احوالا فى احد المعنيين فيجب ان ياتى / فيما يوافقه بمثل الذى شرطه وفيما يخالفه باضداد ذلك قال فقلت انشدنى احسن ما قيل فى ذلك / فقال لا اعرف احسن من قول الشاعر /

فيا عجبا كيف اتفقنا فناصح * وفى ومطوى على الغل غادر /

فجعل بازاء ناصح مطويا على الغل وبازاء وفى غادرا قال وقول الطرماح بن حكيم الطائى /

اسرناهم وانعمنا عليهم * واسقينا دماءهم الترابا /

فما صبروا لبأس بعد [sic] حرب * ولا ادوا [بحسن] يد ثوابا /

فجعل بازاء ان سقوا دماءهم التراب وقاتلوهم ان يصبروا وبازاء ان انعموا عليهم ان يثيبوا قال / فهذه المقابلة قال ابو على سالت على بن هارون عن المقابلة فقال كان يحيى بن على يزعم / ان احسن ما قيل فى المقابلة قول عمرو بن كلثوم / [8b]

ورثنا المجد [41] عن آباء صدق * و[نورثه] اذا متنا بنينا [42] /

فتى تم فيه [ما يسر] صديقه * على ان فيه ما يسوء الاعاديا /

In the first example the differences between the two texts are very slight. In the second example it looks as if the first four lines of Ḥusaynī's text (سئل جماعة ... راويه) are a corrupt version of the beginning of Ḥātimī's chapter in which Ḥātimī

---

41 This line belongs to the famous *Mu'allaqa*. The various editions and commentaries read ورثناهن for ورثنا المجد and نورثها for نورثه. Judging from what remains of the second word in the *Ḥilya* manuscript, it would also be possible to read the second word as نورثها. Nöldeke, *Fünf Mo'allaqāt*, I, 17 (following Barth) puts this line, which is nº 81 in Arnold's edition, after nº 78 and makes the pronoun refer to the suits of armour mentioned in nº 75.

42 The وقول النابغة which one would expect to follow here may have disappeared, since the top of this folio (like that of the other folios up to nº 12) is severely damaged.

observes that ʿAlī b. Hārūn [al-Munajjim] only describes the effect of the figure on the hearer, but fails to offer a technical explanation. It is curious that in the *Naḍra* it is al-Akhfash who offers the lines by Janūb as an example of the *tashīm* and quotes a brief commentary on these lines from the same author, whereas in the *Ḥilya* these are given by ʿAlī b. Hārūn and Abū ʿAlī [al-Ḥātimī] respectively. This may be an indication that Ḥusaynī used a different text in which ʿAlī b. Hārūn was quoted by his *kunya*, Abu ʾl-Ḥasan, thus making possible a confusion between Abu ʾl-Ḥasan ʿAlī [b. Sulaymān al-Akhfash] and Abu ʾl-Ḥasan ʿAlī [b. Hārūn al-Munajjim] (d. 352) [43], and which omitted the *Abū ʿAlī* from *qāla Abū ʿAlī* in the next paragraph. The third example actually contains the name of Ḥātimī, which does not occur in any other chapter of the *Naḍra*. Here one is led to believe that the omission of the name in other chapters (unless one assumes that Ḥusaynī simply wished to claim all these chapters as his own) is due to Ḥusaynī having had no first hand knowledge of the work of his predecessor. The fourth example contains the puzzling reference to Qudāma's family which I mentioned earlier.

Of the chapters in which the dependence of Ḥusaynī on Ḥātimī appears likely four deserve special notice. The first is the chapter on the *ishāra* which clearly borrows from a tradition on Qudāma in the *Ḥilya* [44] without mentioning either the name of Ḥātimī or that of Qudāma. From this one can make an even stronger case for assuming that Ḥusaynī did not use the *Ḥilya* directly [45]. The second is the chapter on the *istithnāʾ*. We have seen that in this chapter Ḥusaynī defines the *istithnāʾ* as *taʾkīd al-madḥ bimā yushbih adh-dhamm*, attributing this definition to Ibn al-Muʿtazz (where, however, it appears as the name of an actual figure). Curiously enough the same phrase occurs at the beginning of the *istithnāʾ* chapter of the *Ḥilya* which opens as follows (fol. 10a) :

احسن ما قيل فى الاستثناء / قال ابو على احسب ان اول من بدأ به النابغة

فاحسن كل الاحسان فى قوله /

ولا عيب فيهم غير ان سيوفهم * بهن فلول من قراع الكتائب /

هذا تاكيد للمدح بما يشبه الذم.[46]

---

43 It is unlikely that Ḥātimī would have meant Akhfash, who died in 315, and therefore lived a little too early to have been the teacher of Ḥātimī who died in 388.

44 See above, p. 19 note 27.

45 The fact that this chapter in the *Naḍra* contains elements found in different chapters in the *Naqd* (the chapters on the *tamthīl* and on the *ishāra*), but in the same chapter in the *Ḥilya*, proves that the material used here by Ḥusaynī goes back ultimately to Ḥātimī, not to Qudāma.

46 Ibn Rashīq (*ʿUmda*, II, 39) makes a somewhat similar statement at the beginning of his *istithnāʾ* chapter. He points out (a) that Ibn al-Muʿtazz uses the term *taʾkīd al-madḥ bimā yushbih adh-dhamm*

The third is the chapter on the *isti'āra* which agrees with the *isti'āra* chapter in the *Ḥilya* in that both contain a report by Ṣūlī about an interview with Ibn al-Mu'tazz during which poetry was discussed. The report also occurs in the *Zahr al-Ādāb* of Ḥuṣrī [47] and there are some differences between the two versions. The fourth is the chapter on the *tashbīh*, a large part of which is taken up by a long and no doubt apocryphal story about a meeting between Aṣma'ī and Hārūn ar-Rashīd in the presence of the Barmacides, Yaḥyā b. Khālid, Ja'far, and Faḍl. Again poetry is the topic of conversation. The story is also quoted in Sharīshī's commentary on the *Maqāmāt* of Ḥarīrī [48] and again the two texts show some differences.

As in the case of Ibn Ṭabaṭabā's *'Iyār* I did not make a detailed analysis of the *Ḥilya*. Nor did I examine the Ḥātimī quotations in works like Ibn Rashīq's *'Umda* and Usāma's *Badī'*. It is therefore quite possible that Ḥusaynī depends on Ḥātimī to a larger degree than I have so far been able to establish. The examples given show that the *Naḍra* may be helpful in supplying missing passages in the *Ḥilya* and in correcting this text of which, as far as I know, only two corrupt and sometimes defective manuscripts exist, but should be used with caution. Among the other authors on the *balāgha* mentioned in the *Naḍra* are 'Alī b. 'Īsā ar-Rummānī (d. 386) from whom Ḥusaynī quotes a definition of the *majāz* (fol. 13b-14a) [49], and 'Abdallāh b. Sinān al-Khafājī (d. 466) whose discussion of the *fasāḥa*, he says, served as a model for his own discussion of the subject in the *Risāla 'Alawiyya* (fol. 13a) [50].

---

instead of *istithnā'*, (b) that the term *istithnā'* is used by Ḥātimī, and (c) that there is a difference between this and the grammatical *istithnā'*. The last statement also occurs in the *Naḍra*, but not in the *Ḥilya*. Once more one is led believe that Ibn Rashīq and Ḥusaynī used a text by Ḥātimī which was different from the *Ḥilya* or not identical with the text we have of this work. It should be noted, however, that Ibn Rashīq quotes the *Ḥilya* by title (*'Umda*, I, 221; II, 215). Perhaps we should read وابن المعتز يسمى هذا تاكيد المدح ... in the *Ḥilya*.

47 Ed. Zakī Mubārak, IV, 114-116 = Muḥ. 'Abdalmun'im Khafājī, *Rasā'il Ibn al-Mu'tazz*, pp. 10-12.

48 Ed. Muḥ. 'Abdalmun'im Khafājī, IV, 170 ff. = p. 54 ff. of the Appendix of an edition by the same scholar of Aṣma'ī's *Fuḥūlat ash-Shu'arā'* (Cairo, 1372/1953).

49 وقال على بن عيسى الرمانى / الحقيقة الدلالة على المعنى من غير جهة الاستعارة والمجاز تحاوز الاصل الى [14a] / الاستعارة. I did not come across the passage in Rummānī's *I'jāz al-Qur'ān*.

50 واما الفصاحة فان الكلام عليها / يحتاج الى شرح طويل يخرج بنا عما نحن بصدده والاقتصار/ فيه غير شاف ولا كاف وقد استوفينا اقسام ذلك فى / الرسالة العلوية وحذونا فيه حذو عبد الله بن سنان الخفاجى / فى صدر كتابه الموسوم بسر الفصاحة.

IV. OTHER INFLUENCES. *ISNĀDS*

Ḥusaynī shows a certain interest in ʿAlid traditions of scholarship as is to be expected in a scholar who was himself a descendant of ʿAlī [1]. We have seen that he makes use of the work of Ibn Ṭabāṭabā al-ʿAlawī. We have also seen that he gave the title *Risāla ʿAlawiyya* to one of his own works which appears to have been a treatise on Mutanabbī and, in addition, may have contained a discussion of rhetoric. His interest in ʿAlid scholarship appears even more clearly from a brief *isnād* on fol. 164b. It contains the names of Ḥusaynī's father and that of a maternal great-uncle of his father, one Muḥ, b. Muḥ. b. ʿUbaydallāh al-ʿAlawī al-Husaynī, whom I have not been able to identify. The same names appear again in an *isnād* on fol. 170a-b. The *Naḍra* also has an uninteresting quotation from Jaʿfar aṣ-Ṣādiq on the term *balīgh* (fol. 11a) [2]. Among the anecdotes in the *Naḍra* there are two dealing with ʿAlid poets. The first, on fols. 194b-197a, attributes political aspirations to the Sharīf ar-Raḍī (d. 406) and mentions some verses addressed to him by Abū Isḥāq aṣ-Ṣābī (d. 384) predicting Raḍī's future greatness which, Ḥusaynī thinks, were not meant seriously. The second, on fols. 205b-206a, describes how one Ḥaydar b. Muḥ. b. ʿUbaydallāh al-ʿAlawī al-Ḥusaynī became the victim of an intrigue which was effected by changing the diacritical points in one of his poems and was put into prison by ʿIzzaddīn Masʿūd, the Atabeg of Mosul. (ruled 572-589) [3]. Ḥusaynī quotes the story on

---

1 The use of the formula عليه السلام after the names of ʿAlī (fols. 158b, 160a-b, 190a, 218a), Jaʿfar aṣ-Ṣādiq (fol. 11a), and Muḥ. al-Bāqir (fol. 232b), and his emphasis on ʿAlī being innocent of the murder of ʿUthmān point to Shīʿite sympathies.

2 وقال جعفر بن محمد الصادق عليه السلام انما سمى البليغ بليغا لانه يبلغ حاجته باهون سعيه.

3 The poem was addressed to [Ṣalāḥaddīn] Yūsuf b. Ayyūb. If the information in the *Naḍra* is correct, the ruler who put Ḥaydar into prison can therefore be no other than ʿIzzaddīn Masʿūd b. Mawdūd (not ʿIzzaddīn Masʿūd b. Arslan Shāh who ruled from 607 till 615). The *Ghāyat al-Ikhtiṣār fi 'l-Buyūtāt al-ʿAlawiyya al-Maḥfūẓa min al-Ghubār* by Tājaddīn al-Ḥusaynī (Najaf, 1963), p. 149, mentions one Kamāladdīn Ḥaydar who was *naqīb* of the ʿAlids in Mosul under ʿImādaddīn Masʿūd b. Mawdūd. It also mentions that he was a poet and composed a *qaṣīda* for Badraddīn Lu'lu'. We have to assume that ʿImādaddīn is a mistake for ʿIzzaddīn (it was ʿIzzaddīn, not his brother, ʿImādaddīn, who ruled in Mosul). Since Badraddīn was born around 575 it is quite possible that this Ḥaydar lived long enough to have addressed a poem to him. The *Amal al-Āmil* of al-Ḥurr al-ʿĀmilī (Baghdad, 1965), II, 108, gives the name as Kamāladdīn Ḥaydar b. Muḥ. b. Zayd b. Muḥ. b. ʿAbdallāh al-Ḥusaynī and quotes a *samāʿ* dating from 570 in which this name occurs.

the authority of his father. Since the purpose of the present article is to bring out the position of the *Naḍra* in relation to other works on rhetoric, I will not discuss these and similar stories (many of them interesting, though of doubtful authenticity) in this context, though I expect to deal with them later. It is not surprising that a number of anecdotes are connected with the history of Ḥusaynī's birthplace, Mosul.

A few words may be said on the *isnāds* in the *Naḍra*. Considering the size of the book and the diversity of the material it contains, Ḥusaynī does not often mention his authorities. There is perhaps no reason to suspect that he did so intentionally in order to suggest to his readers that most of the book was his own work, since in the Introduction he acknowledges the existence of many other works on the subject [4]. On the other hand one may assume that from time to time he wished to impress his readers by his accuracy and to convince them of the reliability of the information he supplied. This he did by quoting occasionally some grammarians and philologists or well known authorities on the *balāgha*, and by giving some *isnāds*. These *isnāds* do not strike one as particularly relevant since none of the statements they introduce are essential to Ḥusaynī's argument. Two of them are perhaps interesting enough to be mentioned. The first appears on fol. 42a-b and runs as follows :

اخبرنى عبد الرحمن الواسطى بقراأتى عليه قال انبأنى ابن خيرون / [42b] عن الجوهرى
وابن المسلمة قالا اخبرنا المرزبانى عن شيوخه / ...

The second is on fol. 229a :

وقريب من هذه الاشعار حكاية اخبرنى / بها عبد الرحمن الدقاق بقراأتى عليه فى
سنة ثلث عشرة / وستمأة قال انبأنى ابن خيرون عن الجوهرى عن المرزبانى / قال
اخبرنى الصولى قال حدثنى يموت بن المزرع قال كان / لمحمد بن الحسن الحصنى ولد ...

Since the two *isnāds* are otherwise identical and, moreover, introduce anecdotes of very similar character (the first deals with a question of rhetorical terminology [5], the second with the use of wrong metaphors), it is likely that ʿAbdarraḥmān al-Wāsiṭī and ʿAbdarrahmān ad-Daqqāq are one and the same person. However,

---

4 Fol. 3b : ... فان / الاستيعاب لما ورد فيه (فى الشعر) وصنف فى معانيه يحتاج الى / تاليف كتب عدة وفراغ له فى طويل من المدة.

5 See below, p. 36.

I have not discovered in any of the biographical dictionaries at my disposal any person by the name of ʿAbdarraḥmān who carries both the *nisba* al-Wāsiṭī and the *laqab* ad-Daqqāq [6]. Nor is there among the ʿAbdarraḥmāns one who carries either the *nisba* or the *laqab* who can be identified with certainty as the authority quoted by Ḥusaynī [7]. The next scholar in the *isnād*, Ibn Khayrūn, is no doubt identical with Abū Manṣūr Muḥ. b. ʿAbdalmalik b. Khayrūn (d. 539) [8]. This Ibn Khayrūn held, according to Ibn al-Jawzī, Dhabahī, Ibn al-Jazarī, and Ibn al-ʿImād an *ijāza* from Abū Muḥ. al-Ḥasan b. ʿAlī al-Jawharī (d. 454). Since Ibn Khayrūn was born in 454 [9], the year in which Jawharī died, he can only have received this *ijāza* upon his birth, a practice which existed as early as the fifth century. That Jawharī studied under Marzubānī (d. 378 or 384) is confirmed by the *Ta'rīkh Baghdād* (III, 135). I have not been able to find the same confirmation for Jawharī's contemporary Ibn al-Muslima. It seems likely that he is identical with one Abū Jaʿfar Muḥ. b. Aḥmad b. Muḥ. b. ʿUmar b. al-Muslima who is mentioned in several collections of biographies [10]. This scholar was born as late as 375 and died in 465, so that the relation between him and Marzubānī may again be fictitious.

The longest *isnād* in the *Naḍra* occupies two half pages on fols. 237b and 238a. It introduces a hadīth illustrating the proverb ان فوق كل طامة طامة والبلاء موكل بالمنطق [11].

---

[6] Ṣafadī, *Wāfī* (MS Bodleian, Arch. Seld. A26, fol. 140a) mentions one ʿAbdarraḥmān b. Abī Bakr b. ʿAbdalbāqī Abū Manṣūr al-Wāsiṭī known as Ibn al-Daqdaq (?), a poet who might well have been a transmitter of the type of traditions Ḥusaynī was interested in. But neither the date of his birth (562), nor the date of his arrival in Baghdad (620), as given by Ṣafadī, would agree with the dates of Ḥusaynī's *isnād*.

[7] One could suggest the Abū Ṭālib ʿAbdarraḥmān b. Muḥ. b. ʿAbdassamīʿ b. Abī Tammām ʿAbdallāh b. ʿAbdassamīʿ al-Hāshimī al-Wāsiṭī mentioned by Ṣafadī, *Wāfī* (MS Bodleian, Arch. Seld. A26), fol., 111a-b; Jazarī, *Ghāyat an-Nihāya*, I, 377 (nº 1607); Ibn Taghrī Bardī, *Nujūm*, VI (Cairo, 1355/1936), 260; Ibn al-ʿImād, *Shadhadrāt*, V, 94-95, who was born in 538, one year before the death of Ibn Khayrūn, and died in 621. But from his biography it would seem that he was more interested in theological than in literary studies.

[8] See Ibn al-Jawzī, *Muntaẓam*, X, 115; Dhahabī, *ʿIbar*, IV, 109; idem, *Mushtabih* (ed. de Jong), p. 194; Ibn; al-Jazarī, *Ghāyat an-Nihāya*, II, 192 (nº 3209); Ibn Taghrī Bardī, *Nujūm*, V (Cairo, 1353/1935), V, 276; Nuʿaymī, *Dāris*, I, 408, 416, and 484; Ibn al-ʿImād, *Shadharāt*, IV, 125.

[9] So Ibn al-Jawzī, who also specifies that he was born in the month of Rajab. According to the *Ta'rīkh Baghdād*, VII, 393, Jawharī died in Dhu 'l-Qaʿda of the same year. Other biographies of Jawharī in Samʿānī, *Ansāb* (ed. Margoliouth), 144a; Ibn al-Jawzī, *Muntaẓam*, VIII, 227-228; Ibn al-Athīr, *Lubāb* (Cairo, 1357), I, 255; Dhahabī, *ʿIbar*, III, 231-232; Ibn Kathīr, *Bidāya*, XII, 88; Ibn al-Jazarī, *Ghāyat an-Nihāya*, I, 225 (nº 1023); Ibn Taghrī Bardī, *Nujūm*, V, 70-71; Nuʿaymī, *Dāris*, I, 484; Ibn al-ʿImād, *Shadharāt*, III, 292.

[10] See *Ta'rīkh Baghdād*, I, 356; Samʿānī, *Ansāb*, 530a; Ibn al-Jawzī, *Muntaẓam*, VIII, 282; Ibn al-Athīr, *Lubāb*, II, 138; Ṣafadī, *Wāfī*, II, 83; Dhahabī, *ʿIbar*, III, 259-260; idem, *Mushtabih*, p. 481; Ibn Taghrī Bardī, *Nujūm*, V, 94; Ibn al-ʿImād, *Shadharāt*, III, 323.

[11] See Mufaḍḍal b. Salama, *Kitāb al-Fākhir* (ed. ʿAbdalʿalīm aṭ-Ṭaḥāwī), p. 237; Maydānī, *Majmaʿ*, *al-Amthāl* (Cairo, 1379/1959), I, 18; Freytag, *Proverbia*, I, 19.

It contains the name of the Ibn al-Baqqāl whom, as I have said earlier, Ḥusaynī qualifies as his teacher [12], and also many other names which, as far as they are identifiable, do not call for special attention. Three names are so much abbreviated that they might be hard to identify. This and the fact that elsewhere he abbreviates or omits *isnāds* that must have appeared in full in works by earlier authorities from whom he borrowed (such as Marzubānī and Ḥātimī), prove that Ḥusaynī's approach to his subject was hardly systematic either by the standards of his own time or by ours.

---

[12] See above, p. 9.

V. TWO NOTES ON THE *BADĪʿ* TERMINOLOGY

To end this brief survey, two passages deserve to be quoted, since they are of particular interest for the early history of the *badīʿ* terminology. As I have pointed out earlier, there are several such passages, but since they were in all probability taken over from Ḥātimī's *Ḥilyat al-Muḥāḍara* (or from a similar work by the same author) they should rather be quoted in a forthcoming article on the two existing manuscripts of this work. The first passage is on fol. 42a-b and occurs in the chapter on the *tajnīs*. It is introduced by the *isnād* given in the preceding section [1] and quotes the great-grandson of Jarīr, ʿUmāra b. ʿAqīl (still alive under Mutawakkil, 232-247) [2] as using the term *raddāt* instead of *tajnīs* :

ومن مليح هذا القسم من التجنيس (i. e. المجنّس المتمّم) قول الطائى / اخبرنى عبد الرحمن الواسطى بقراأتى عليه قال انبأنى ابن خيرون /[42b] عن الجوهرى وابن المسلمة قالا اخبرنا المرزبانى عن شيوخه / قال استنشد عمارة بن عقيل بن بلال بن جرير اصحاب ابى تمام شيئا من شعره فانشدوه /

اذا الجمت يوما لجيم وحولها * بنو الحصن نجل المحصنات النجائب /
فان المنايا والصوارم والقنا * اقاربهم فى الروع دون الاقارب /
اذا الخيل جابت قسطل النقع صدّعوا * صدور العوالى فى صدور الكتائب /
يمدّون من ايد عواص عواصم * تصول باسياف قواض قواضب [3] /

فقال عمارة لله دره كان رداته / ردات جرير فسمى التجنيس ردات.

---

1 See above, p. 33.

2 See *GAL*, G I, 79; S I, 122.

3 See Abū Tammām, *Dīwān* (ed. Muḥ. ʿAbduh ʿAzzām), I, 213 and 215. This quotation is taken from a famous poem on Abū Dulaf al-Qāsim b. ʿĪsā al-ʿIjlī (d. 225 or 226). For a discussion of the poem and

The second passage occurs on fol. 62b and states that the term *amthāl* was used instead of *istiʿāra* by "the ancients". It runs as follows :

باب الاستعارة / الاستعارة من اشرف صنعة الكلام واجلها وكان القدماء / يسمونها الامثال فيقولون فلان كثير الامثال ولقبها / بالاستعارة الزم لانه اعم ولان الامثال كلها ليس تجرى / مجرى الاستعارة الا ترى قول السليك بن السلكة وقد / وقع عليه رجل وهو نائم فضغطه السليك فحبق الرجل فقال / السليك اضرطا وانت الاعلى [4] فارسلها مثلا وقد اورد / الشيء على حقيقته.

There is good reason to question some of the statements in the *Naḏra*, especially where no authorities are quoted, as in this second tradition. In this case, however, Ḥusaynī may be correct, though I know of only one place where the term *mathal* is clearly used in the sense of *istiʿāra*. It occurs in Abū Muḥ. al-Qāsim b. al-Anbārī's commentary on the *Mufaḍḍaliyyāt* (ed. Lyall, p. 855-856) and goes back to Aṣmaʿī [5] :

واذا المنية انشبت اظفارها * الفيت كل تميمة لا تنفع

قال الضبى قال الاصمعى هذا مثل وليس للمنية اظفار ... [p. 856] وانما قال انشبت اظفارها تشبيها بالسبع لا تفارقه حتى تقتله.

I did not find his assertion that the term *raddāt* was used as a synonym of *tajnīs* confirmed in any other text.

---

for further references see ʿAbdalqāhir al-Jurjānī, *Asrār* (ed. Ritter), p. 18, nº 20 and note; Ritter, *Die Geheimnisse der Wortkunst des ʿAbdalqāhir al-Jurjānī*, p. 33-34 and note. This type of *tajnīs* is more commonly called *nāqiṣ* or *muṭarraf*, cf. Mehren, *Die Rhetorik der Araber*, p. 157-158; *EI*, s.v. TADJNĪS.

4 See Ibn Qutayba, *Shiʿr* (ed. de Goeje), p. 215; Mufaḍḍal aḍ-Ḍabbī, *Amthāl al-ʿArab* (Istanbul, 1300/1883), p. 13; Maydānī, *Majmaʿ al-Amthāl*, I. 420; Freytag, *Proverbia*, II, 6-7.

5 Bāqillānī (d. 403) suggests that Aṣmaʿī also knew the term *istiʿāra*; see *Iʿjāz al-Qurʾān* (ed. Aḥmad Ṣaqr), p. 108 (transl. by von Grunebaum, *A Tenth-Century Document of Arabic Literary Criticism*, p. 7).

Drukkerij Orientaliste, p.v.b.a., Leuven (België)